Museum of Fine Arts, Boston
ABC

Florence Cassen Mayers

Harry N. Abrams, Inc.
Publishers
New York

For my children, Lela and Dara, and my husband, Bob,
and for my mother

Editor: Sheila Franklin
Designer: Florence Cassen Mayers

Library of Congress Catalog Card Number: 86–70238
ISBN 0–8109–1847–1

Design copyright © 1986 Florence Cassen Mayers
All photographs copyright © the Museum of Fine Arts, Boston

Published in 1986 by Harry N. Abrams, Incorporated, New York
All rights reserved. No part of the contents of this book may be
reproduced without the written permission of the publishers

Times Mirror Books

Printed and bound in Japan

Title page:
Harriet Boardman (American)
Sampler Embroidery
1804. Silk embroidery on linen, 15¾ x 11''
Gift of Mrs. Samuel Cabot

Introduction

This ABC is unique and beautiful because each letter of the alphabet is illustrated with a painting, sculpture, musical instrument, or work of decorative art from the rich and varied holdings of the Museum of Fine Arts, Boston.

The book has been designed to appeal to children of all ages. For the preschool child, it provides a novel way to learn the alphabet; for the older child, it is a true first artbook, containing masterpieces from a museum world-famous for its Early American, Asiatic, and Impressionist collections. Preschool children turning the pages of this book will immediately recognize "Boy" for B, "Jar" for J, "King" for K. They need not know that these are masterworks by superb artists in order to delight in and enjoy them. Older children, just becoming aware of art and museums, will find this book an exciting way to get a first glimpse of the Museum's vast art treasures. Through the images on these pages, art becomes accessible and fun. Children will be fascinated to learn that things as friendly and familiar as quilts and teakettles or as varied and exotic as harps and mummies can all be part of a museum collection.

If you live near the Museum, take this book along as a guide the next time you visit with your children. Encourage them to search for their favorite works, to hunt for Steinlen's *Cats*, for example, or Renoir's *Dance at Bougival*. Soon your children will be guiding you.

What more wonderful way could there possibly be for a child to learn the ABCs of language *and* art than through this book and this collection?

Armchair

Armchair
American, Philadelphia or Chester County, Pennsylvania
1750–85. Maple, 46¹⁄₁₆ x 22⅞ x 17"
Bequest of Dudley Leavitt Pickman

Bb

Boy

Cc

Théophile Alexandre Steinlen (French, 1859–1923)
Cats
1894. Hand-colored lithograph, 23¼ x 19⅛″
Bequest of W. G. Russell Allen

Cats

Dd

Dancers

Ee

Eagle

Wilhelm Schimmel (American, 1817–1890)
Young Eagle with Outspread Wings
1860–90. Wood, painted and varnished, height 7³⁄₁₆″,
wingspread 12¾″
M. and M. Karolik Collection

Ff

Fruit

Fish

Gg

Giraffe

Anonymous (American)
Giraffe
1836. Watercolor, 12⅛ x 12½"
M. and M. Karolik Collection

Hh

Harp

Single-Action Pedal Harp
Maker: Holzman, Paris, France
About 1770. Pine, gilt gesso, oil paint, iron and gut, height 63"
Leslie Lindsey Mason Collection of Musical Instruments
(formerly the Galpin Collection)

Ii

Island

Ogata Kōrin (Japanese, 1658–1716)
Scenic View at Matsushima
Edo period, early 18th century. Two panels from a six-panel
folding screen: ink, colors and gold on paper, entire screen 61¼ x 145¾″
Fenollosa-Weld Collection

Jj

Jar

Jar
Chinese
T'ang dynasty, 8th century A.D.
Three-color glazed earthenware, height 11″
Charles B. Hoyt Collection

Kk

King

Anonymous (Japanese)
European King and Members of His Court
Momoyama period, about 1601–14. One panel from a
six-panel folding screen: ink, colors and gold on paper,
each panel 50 x 22"
Fenollosa-Weld Collection

Ll

Letter

Mm

Mummy case

Mummy Case of the House Mistress and Songstress of Amun Tabes,
Wife of the Barber of the Temple of Amun, Nes-Ptah
Egyptian
22nd–25th dynasties, about 940–660 B.C. Cartonnage, length 65¾"
Gift of C. Granwell Way

Nn

Nest

John James Audubon (American, born Santo Domingo, 1785–1851),
after Robert Havell, Jr.
Yellow-Breasted Chat (detail), from *The Birds of America* (plate 137)
1827–38. Hand-colored aquatint, 28 x 40"
Gift of William Hooper, 1921

Oo

Owl

Cornelius Bloemaert the Younger
(Netherlandish, 1603–after 1683),
after Hendrik Bloemaert
The Wise Owl
17th century. Engraving, 14 x 18"
George Reed Nutter Fund

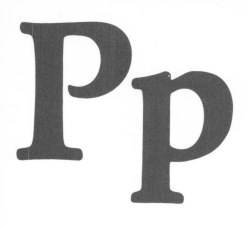

Peacock

Peacock Weathervane
American
Mid-19th century. Copper, height 19″, length 37″
M. and M. Karolik Collection

Quilt

Celestine Bacheller (American, 1840–1922)
Quilt with Scenes of Wyoma, Massachusetts
1850–1900. Various embroidered fabrics, 74¼ x 57"
Gift of Mr. and Mrs. Edward J. Healy in memory
of Mrs. Charles O'Malley

Rr

Rabbits

Henri-Charles Guérard (French, 1846–1897)
Rabbits
1893. Woodcut, 12⅞ x 9¼"
George Reed Nutter Fund

Ss

Store

John Frederick Peto (American, 1854–1907)
The Poor Man's Store
1885. Oil on canvas and wood, 36 x 25½"
M. and M. Karolik Collection

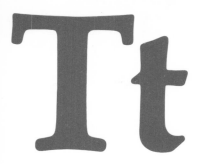

Tt

Teakettle

Jacob Hurd (American, 1702/3–1758)
Teakettle on a Stand
1730–40. Silver, height (including handle)
14⅜″, depth 7½″
Gift of Esther Lowell Abbott in memory
of her mother, Esther Lowell Cunningham,
granddaughter of James Russell Lowell

Uu

Umbrellas

Vv

Violinist

Hilaire-Germain-Edgar Degas (French, 1834–1917)
The Violinist
About 1879. Charcoal and white chalk, 18⅞ x 12″
William Francis Warden Fund

Ww

Washington

Gilbert Stuart (American, 1755–1828)
George Washington (detail)
1796. Oil on canvas, 48 x 37"
Museum of Fine Arts, Boston,
and The National Portrait Gallery,
Smithsonian Institution, Washington, D.C.

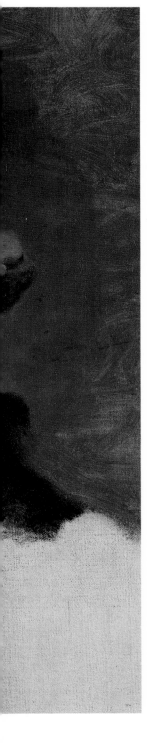

X-ray

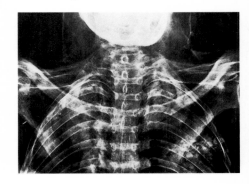

X-ray of the Skull and Rib Cage of the
Mummy of the Offerer in Thebes,
Ankhpefhor
Egyptian
Late dynastic or Ptolemaic periods,
about 664–30 B.C.
Courtesy of the Egyptian Department,
Museum of Fine Arts, Boston, and
Brigham and Women's Hospital, Boston

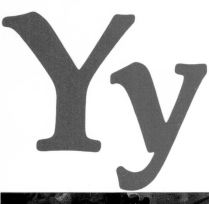

Yy

Youngsters

Jefferson Gauntt (American, 1806–1864)
Two Children
1843. Oil on canvas, 50 x 40″
M. and M. Karolik Collection

Zz

Zigzag

Court Girdle, or *Patka* (detail)
North Indian (Mughal)
Early 18th century. Brocade, silk embroidered
with silk and silver-gilt thread, 139¾ x 28"
Gift of John Goelet